# Once u

A fairytale r

## By Tom Leimdorfer

QUAKERS

First printed 1992; new edition printed January 2014.

Quaker Peace & Social Witness, Friends House, 173–177 Euston Road, London, NW1 2BJ.

ISBN: 978-1-907123-57-3

A Large-print edition of this booklet is available; please contact the publications manager on 020 7663 1162 or email publications@quaker.org.uk.

For further information you can contact Isabel Cartwright, Peace Education Programme Manager, Quaker Peace & Social Witness (QPSW).

Friends House Euston Road London NW12BJ, Tel: 020 7663 1087
Email: isabelc@quaker.org.uk, www.quaker.org.uk.

# Contents

# Introduction

'...and they lived happily ever after.'

Quite possibly, but not before they learnt to solve some of life's most difficult problems. Fairy stories have many facets. They show heroic enterprise to overcome great adversity or to perform seemingly impossible tasks. They show that life is not always fair; some meet with good luck and others with great misfortune. They also show that conflict is an integral part of life. People are different, they have differing wants and needs. Clashes of interest are inevitable.

Nor is conflict always a bad thing. It can release creative energy, lead to the birth of new ideas. It can bring people together in a joint enterprise to find a solution, even if they were on opposing sides. It can also be very destructive and violent. Indeed, many fairytales include a violent ending (usually reserved for the 'baddy'), showing that doing away with your opponent is one extreme option. It is not surprising that many fairytales have acquired a variety of different endings as people searched for alternative solutions to the problem.

Fairytales hold a mirror to many of our contemporary problems. If we look carefully, we see reflections of ethnic conflict, petty crime, problems of debt, urban expansion, family breakdown, poverty, bullying, jealousy and intolerance.

The particular angle chosen for each conflict resolution exercise is not supposed to represent 'the truth' of the original fairy story. It is merely one facet of it, chosen to throw light on some of the problems we see around us today. The story is adapted, often to show how matters may have looked from the point of view of the less sympathetic characters.

Problem-solving should be fun. Each of the exercises can be taken at several different levels. They can be used for role-play or for discussing and analysing problems. The text can be simplified for young children and treated at the level of the story itself or it can be used for looking at aspects of social problems in greater depth. It is surprising how children as young as nine or ten will often spot subtleties in the conflict situation which adults fail to see! They can also be more creative in suggesting different options, when adults may be conditioned to fix their sights on one course of action.

This short book is not intended as a training manual on problem-solving and mediation techniques. The main framework and basic techniques are pointed out in the later sections and lists of useful publications and organisations are given for those who would like further training in mediation skills. It might be more logical to start with the theory, but life is not like that. We meet problems and try to solve them with the tools at our disposal. If we fail, we may need to look around for new tools or seek help. Theory becomes useful when we see the need for it.

Quaker Peace & Social Witness (QPSW) is a centre for local, national and international Quaker action for peace and justice with a commitment to nonviolent social change. Its work strives to reflect and express Quaker testimonies to peace and nonviolence, simplicity, equality and community, truth and integrity. The Peace Education Programme helps children and young people discover the wonder and beauty within themselves, nurturing inner peace. It supports the development of the attitudes, values, skills to respond to conflict creatively, so encouraging inter-personal peace. It further encourages children to examine the root causes of violence and war, to explore the possibilities of peace at community, national and international levels.

This publication was written by Tom Leimdorfer and first published in 1992, when he was working as Education Adviser for Quaker Peace & Service (now QPSW). Tom came to England as a teenage refugee from Hungary in 1956. His career included being a science teacher and a secondary headteacher. Following his time at Friends House, he worked in special educational needs for a local authority and Family Adviser for Mencap. He was elected a local authority councilor in 2003.

The illustration on page 33 is by Ian Duncan; other illustrations are by Julianna Mrena and Judit Pécskõi, who were school students in Szolnok, Hungary. 'Big Grey and Little Red' and 'Cindy' were adapted from versions devised by Sue Bowers of the Kingston Friends Workshop Group and the idea of 'Goldie and the Browns' came from Val Major, formerly of Bristol Mediation. The original publication was actively supported by Pax Christi, a gospel-based, lay-inspired peacemaking movement, which strives to help the Church to proclaim and make peace especially through witness and action by its members.

This edition has been expanded with additional material from Isabel Cartwright, Peace Education Programme Manager, Quaker Peace & Social Witness (QPSW) with help and support from CRESST – an organisation in Sheffield which run sessions in non-violent conflict resolution, and trains children and young people to become peer mediators (www.cresst.org.uk) and Turning the Tide, a QPSW programme which promotes the understanding and use of nonviolence to help us become more effective (www.turning-the-tide.org).

Friends House, Euston Road, London NW1 2BJ, Tel: 0207 663 1087.

Email: isabelc@quaker.org.uk.

# Big Grey and Little Red

We all know about the unfortunate experience of Little Red Riding Hood. There seems to be no doubt that the Wolf in the story behaved extremely badly. But why was that 'Big Grey' so hungry that he risked coming amongst humans? Our Big Grey could be a wolf ... but could be human too!

## Big Grey

You are Big Grey. Your ancestors have lived in the forest for many generations. The forest used to be much bigger and your ancestors used to roam freely and find plenty of food in the forest. There was a small village at the edge of the forest, but the settlers who lived there did not trouble your tribe and you had very little to do with them.

It is very different now. The village grew and grew into a large town and much of the forest has been cut down. The settlers have been hunting the Big Greys and there are not many of you left. There is also very little food left to find in what remains of the forest. So you are forced to look for food at the edges of the town and steal from the settlers. Life has become very dangerous.

Yesterday, you met this young settler called Little Red. She was carrying some delicious food in a basket, going along the path the settlers built through what was once part of the forest, but is now one of their 'parks'. You asked her for some food, but she refused rudely. You gathered that she was visiting her grandmother in the old part of the town. So you ran ahead, quickly shut the old woman in the cupboard and took her place in the bed, hurriedly putting on some of her clothes. When Little Red arrived, you tried to get the food from her, but she must have recognised you because she screamed, made an awful fuss so that an angry crowd of settlers armed with nasty weapons came after you and you were very lucky to escape – still starving.

Luckily, it seems as if there is some kind of Mediation Service which has been set up in the town to help sort out arguments. You think that this might give you a chance to put your side of the story and they have invited you to come along with a guarantee of safe passage, so you go along to meet the Mediator and Little Red.

## Little Red

You live in a town which has been built near the edge of a forest. You live with your mother who has to work very hard to get enough money to feed you both and to pay for the other necessary things. Your grandmother lives in the old part of the town, which was originally just a small village. She is a very independent old lady and wants to live in the small cottage where she lived all her life. She is getting frail and cannot cook for herself every day, so you take her one meal a day, which your mother has prepared. The only way to her house (other than going a very long way round) takes you through the park which was once part of the forest. You have heard that Big Greys still live in the forest and sometimes wander into the park. You are rather frightened, but dare not tell your mother as she has enough troubles already.

Yesterday, as you were going to grandmother's house, suddenly this Big Grey

came up to you and asked for food. Naturally you tried to get rid of him, but you must have said something about where you were going. When you got to grandmother's house, she was in bed and looked very strange. She asked you odd questions and was very eager to grab the food. As she reached towards you, you suddenly recognised Big Grey. Of course, you screamed for help and were very relieved when some builders and gardeners who worked next door rushed in with their tools and chased the Big Grey away.

You have been invited to talk to Big Grey in the presence of the new

Mediation Service which tries to sort out problems in the town. You have heard that Big Greys are dying out as they do not have enough food in the forest. But you are mainly interested in knowing that you can safely deliver food for grandmother.

## Mediator

You live in a town which has been built near the edge of a forest. The town has grown and the forest has shrunk. The Big Greys which live in the forest are also much reduced in number as they find less food and have been hunted by the town dwellers. They have recently become a nuisance and even a danger to the townsfolk as they come into the parks (which used to be part of the forest) and even to the streets near the edge of the town in search of food.

There is a conservation lobby in the town which advocates measures to preserve the traditional life of the Big Greys. There is also a 'safe streets' lobby which wants strong measures to protect the townsfolk from the Big Greys.

Yesterday there was an incident when a Big Grey slunk up to a young girl named Little Red who was walking through the park to take food to her elderly grandmother who lives on her own. He asked for food, she was frightened and ran away. On entering her grandmother's house, she started talking to the figure in the bedroom whom she assumed to be her grandmother, only to find that it was Big Grey who (as it turned out) had shut the old lady in a cupboard and was now trying to trick Little Red into giving him the food. She shrieked for help and some neighbours, armed with garden tools, chased the Big Grey away. Both Big Grey and Little Red have agreed to come to the town Mediation Service.

These are brief notes for a mediator in this, or any other dispute. A fuller description of the mediation process is given later in this book.

- You explain to both sides that you are not part of the legal system. You are not a judge, nor an arbitrator. It is not your job to decide the rights and wrongs in the conflict or to decide what should happen next. Your job is to help people in conflict to come to some agreement themselves, to decide on action which would improve the situation for both of them.

- Try to put them at their ease. Try to agree on ground rules (listening to each other, not interrupting etc.).

- Try to structure the process, using the basic steps of mediation:

  1. What has happened? What is the problem? Find a way of stating the problem so that both parties agree to the wording. This means that it may have to be a statement like: 'There is a disagreement about...'

  2. Give each party a chance to say how he/she feels about the matter. Try to rephrase any accusations (e.g. 'you/he/she are/is) as I statements' (e.g. 'I feel upset/angry because...'). Try to identify fears: '...so am I right that you are afraid that...'

  3. Give each party a chance to say what would be her/his ideal solution and also what are her/his basic needs. Try to find out what is vital and what is less important to each side.

  4. Encourage both sides to think of as many action steps as possible in this situation and to discuss the pros and cons of each option. Can they pick out any which suits them both and on which they can agree?

Throughout the process, try to build more trust. Thank each party for making any cooperative steps. Do not try to browbeat either side for the sake of forcing a solution. The conflict may be complex and may not be resolved at one stroke. It may be more realistic to aim for an agreement on some simple action steps than for a grand scheme which will solve everything.

# Goldie and the Browns

Why was 'Goldilocks' wandering around and why was she so hungry and tired that she risked entering a strange house? She was clearly in the wrong, trespassing and probably committing a crime. Did she know it was wrong, was she so desperate that she was past caring? Was she an unemployed young person, a traveller, an asylum seeker?

There are a number of circumstances which make people flee from their surroundings. Those with money and good connections have the option to flee and start a new life in ways which society finds acceptable. It is very different for those who have no such resources. Wherever they go, they are strangers and represent a threat to the established way of life of those already there. They arrive with nothing and this challenges others to share their resources (jobs, space, money) or to see them starve. It is a conflict which induces much fear and inflames passions.

## Goldie

You felt you could no longer survive at home. There was little to go round, you were unwanted, picked on, threatened. There was no place of safety and nobody you could trust to help you. So you left, carrying just a few personal possessions in a bag. You have had a long journey; you are tired, hungry and thirsty. Several people have refused to help you find somewhere to stay.

Then you came across this house in the woods. The door was ajar, there seemed to be nobody around, it was a warm and comfortable place. The people who lived there obviously were not short of anything. There was food on the table. One bowl was very hot and you burnt your tongue, but another was cooler and you ate your fill. You stretched and swung back on the chair, which collapsed! You felt exhausted, sleepy with the warmth and the luxury of a full stomach, you looked for a bed and found one that felt just right and fell fast asleep.

You did not sleep long. You were woken by angry voices. The owners (the Brown family) returned and quickly found you. They looked ready to beat you up, so you ran away. However, you were afraid that they might report you to the police, so you went back and tried to explain your situation. They had calmed down a bit, but were still angry and told you to go away. 'You are not our problem' said Mr. Brown. You spend the night sleeping rough, just outside their fence. Next morning they see you there and they are angry and threaten to call the police. Then Mr. Brown says that you should go with him to the Advice Bureau in the town. You suspect that this is just a ploy to get you off their hands, but you agree to go.

## Ted Brown

You are hardworking, careful with money and trying to make sure that your family will never go short. You have a comfortable house, but you are always thinking of new improvements. You have chosen to live on the edge of a quiet town by some lovely woods, a good neighbourhood of people similar to yourself. However, the town has had some problems lately with all kinds of vagrants, begging and wanting food and shelter. There have been break-ins and other incidents of crime. Some of your neighbours have invested in elaborate security devices. You have had no trouble... till yesterday.

Yesterday you cooked the supper, while your wife and small son went for a walk by the river. Everything was ready and served out and they were still not back, so you went to find them and get them to hurry. You forgot to lock the door, but you only expected to be out for a couple of minutes.

You could hardly believe your eyes when you returned with your wife and son. You had an intruder! The food on the table has been eaten, your son's small chair was broken and then you found this vagrant in his bed. You could feel your blood boil with anger! She looked filthy and used abusive language as she ran away.

You were just wondering about calling the police, when she had the cheek to come back and tell you her hard luck story and beg for food and shelter. You felt a bit sorry for her, but were still very angry and you couldn't see why you should have anything to do with her problems and told her to go away. The next morning she is still there, obviously having spent the night sleeping rough just outside your garden fence. You first threaten to call the police, and then tell her to go to see the Citizen's Advice Bureau in town. You agree to take her there as this seems to be the only way to get her away from your house.

# Citizen's Advice Bureau worker

You live in a town which has a good deal of civic pride. The majority of the inhabitants are quite well off and the poorer sections of the community have traditionally been well looked after. There have always been problems, of course, but in the past the established ways of dealing with most of these have avoided crisis situations. Recently, however, the town has faced an influx of homeless vagrants for whom there is no provision. There are now fewer and fewer council homes and the waiting list has local young families and elderly folk on it. With the influx of homeless people has come begging on the streets and break-ins and squatting. Strong police action is urged by some, while others would like to see a hostel for the homeless. That is something the council can ill-afford at the moment and it might also encourage more newcomers.

This morning Mr. Brown, a well-respected local citizen, has brought a young girl to see you. His family found her in their house yesterday. Without any invitation, she slunk in, ate some of their food, broke the child's chair (probably by accident), then went to sleep in a bedroom. They threw her out, but she slept rough near their house and appeared again in the morning. She is clearly homeless and in need of some shelter. What can you advise? First, you need to hear their full story and their feelings. You have no magic wand, but you can ask them to suggest possible ways forward. You know full well that the Browns have the means to give shelter to someone at least temporarily, but you dare not suggest it. After all, your own family would be far from pleased with having to share your home with a stranger.

# Hansel and the Elderly Widow

The story of Hansel and Gretel takes up the theme of the many internal and external pressures which can build up to family breakdown. The external factors are poverty caused by unemployment, scarcity of food in some societies, recessions in others. The internal stresses can come from conflict between adults and teenagers, problems in relationships between children of a first marriage and the second wife/husband. If any of the children leave home early as a result of such stresses, they often find themselves in a very hostile world. It may well appear to present them with a choice between suffering neglect and oppression or resorting to crime.

## Husband

You have always had to work hard for your living doing joinery and other building work. There were times when it was a good trade, but in recent years there was little work around and you have found it harder and harder to make ends meet. You are in debt and there isn't enough food to go round, no matter how carefully you shop. Your first wife died when your two children were quite young and you since remarried. Your second wife met and married you when things were going quite well and she resents your extreme poverty now. She is also very hard on the youngsters, especially when they want things other teenagers take for granted. There are always quarrels at home. Hansel, the older one ran away from home once after such a quarrel, but he was soon back and things were alright for a while.

Then things really started to go wrong. Your wife and son had a tremendous row and she insisted that she would not have him in the house any longer. He packed his bag and decided to hitchhike to the big city to try to find work. You gave him what little money and food you could spare and told

him to write and tell you where he is and what he is doing. You heard
nothing for a long time and you were very worried. Then you had a brief
note to say that he had been sleeping rough and could not find a proper
job. He was now working for someone he referred to as 'the old witch',
who exploited him terribly, but at least gave him enough food to eat. Then
suddenly you had this letter from the police to say that he was in a remand
centre awaiting trial for causing grievous bodily harm to an elderly widow.

## Wife

You came from a large family where life was always hard. You left school
as soon as you could in order to find a job and since then you always had
to make your own way in the world. The man you met and fell in love with
was quite a lot older than you. He was a widower with two children. He was
doing alright at the time, he had a good job and the children seemed fine,
you felt you were getting on with them. You hoped to have a child of your
own, but this never happened. Then your husband lost his job and couldn't
find work, so there could be no question of having an extra child anyway.
The money situation got tighter and tighter and then the hardware shop
where you were working had to close. You now depend on benefits and are
getting further into debt.

Meanwhile you could not stop your family from spending money and being
wasteful. Your husband still had to have his pint of beer; he would still keep
buying things for the little girl Gretel whenever she asked ('all my friends
have...'). Worst of all, was the boy Hansel. He had a huge appetite; he was
smoking and drinking when he could get away with it. You always had to
check up on him where money was concerned. He would 'borrow' money
under one pretext and use it for something else. He always complained that
you were stingy. His father did nothing to discipline him and get him to be
more responsible.

The rows with the boy were getting worse and affecting your marriage. The
boy had a short temper and you were afraid that he might even hit you one
day.

He was the same age as you were when you left home. Here he was with
no job, just spending money you didn't have! You'd had enough. You told
him to get out. You hoped that might make a man of him. Now he is in big
trouble. He is in a prison remand centre for having assaulted and badly hurt
an old woman he was working for. You feel your husband blames you for
what has happened.

# Hansel

You are seventeen years old and the world is against you. Your mother died when you were only eleven. Your father remarried and you remember quite liking your stepmother at first. The past two years have been terrible. Your father lost his job, you were not getting on well at school and there were more and more rows at home about money. You could not do any of the things your friends were doing without being shouted at by your stepmother. The odd cigarette or drink was a major crime, if you bought a DVD or tried to get money for a decent pair of trainers she made you feel as if it were your fault if the family starved. She was on at you about taking food from the fridge or leaving lights on or a tap running or using too much loo paper – it went on and on. Once you ran away to a friend. After that you talked things over and you tried and she seemed nicer, but then it all started worse than ever.

You left school, had no job, the only training scheme you were offered was awful and it was an awkward place to get to anyway. So you were hanging around and the rows got worse till your stepmother said she would no longer have you in the house. You decided to leave and try to find work in the city, so you packed your bag, took the money your Dad gave you and hitched to the city. For a while you could get nothing – no work, only temporary shelters to stay in or sleeping rough. Then you saw in a shop window an advert for someone to do household chores. It turned out that the old woman wanted cleaning, gardening, everything done, for just feeding you and some pocket money. It was better than nothing, but she kept complaining about your work, kept calling you names. When she referred to your mother, you lost your temper.

You don't know what came over you, you pushed her hard, and she fell against the stove. You panicked and ran away. The neighbour found her badly burnt. Now you are in a remand centre facing charges for assault and causing grievous bodily harm.

# Elderly Widow

You live on your own in the big city. Your husband died many years ago and you have to make do on your pension. You are beginning to feel that some of the jobs of keeping the house clean and the garden going are getting too much for you. You always managed on your own and never paid for people to work for you – could never afford to anyway. You have good neighbours, but they are getting on in years as well and you cannot expect them to help.

You thought you would try to advertise for some household help. The woman who first answered the advert wanted far too much money. Then this lad called Hansel came to the door. You had your doubts, but he didn't look a bad sort and he was clearly hungry and eager to work. He was not much good; you kept having to ask him to do things again properly. You thought he would be grateful to work for food and a pound an hour, but he grumbled about you being mean.

You gathered that he left home to look for work; you suspected that there had been something of a row. Anyway, his parents didn't do much of a job bringing him up. You said something to that effect, when suddenly the boy became violent. You are not even sure what happened. He hit you and pushed you against the stove, then left you lying there. A neighbour heard you scream and called the ambulance. When you explained what happened, she also called the police. You are recovering from burns and bruises in hospital. Apart from the pain, you are badly shaken, confused and not sure if you can go home and manage on your own. You feel sure that you dare not advertise for help again.

# Three Little Pigs

According to the original story the wicked wolf was all set to eat up the sweet innocent little pigs. Two of them did not build strong enough dwellings to keep the wolf out, but the wise third pig had a well-built house which in some versions saved all three pigs, in other versions just himself. But what on earth were those pigs doing in the forest in the first place?

## Wolf

You live in the forest and have lived there for as long as you can remember. It is a beautiful forest away from the bustle and dirt of town life. You want to keep it as it is and you don't mind 'living rough' in nature. You know that people think of you as being odd, try to avoid you, and call you 'the wolf'.

Now this new development has started in the forest for holiday homes. They have already cut down some of the most beautiful trees. You went to object, but did not know how to go about it, got angry and lost your temper, and they just laughed at you. Townsfolk, who make such a mess of natural surroundings you think of them as 'pigs', are buying up plots of land and your forest home is fast disappearing. Three of them have already arrived. One has pitched up a gaudy tent, one has put up a wooden summer-house and one seems to be building a small fortress with fenced garden round a brick-built suburban house. They are all noisy people who play loud unpleasant music. You are very angry, frustrated, do not know what to do about it, and feel violent hatred towards those who are ruining your way of life.

## Adventurous camper

You are getting rather tired of the routine daily life in the big town and feel ready for some adventure. You have some savings and have bought a plot of land on a new development of holiday homes in the forest. You cannot afford to build a proper house on it, and in any case, you think that camping would be more fun, to start with at least.

You have been warned that there may be some odd people living rough in that area of the forest - one of them, nicknamed 'the wolf', made quite a scene at the offices of the developers - but you think they are likely to be harmless enough. After all, you are not hurting anyone by enjoying yourself in the forest: making barbecues, listening to your music in the open air and sampling the 'simple life'!

## Summer House Owner

You had been saving up for a summer house for a long time. Luckily, a new holiday development started just when you could afford a reasonable sized, wooden summer house. It came in kit form and you feel you have made a reasonable of job of putting it up. You are ready improving your site, by chopping down a few trees to make a wooden fence round your plot and you love working outdoors, lighting bonfires and listening to your music.

You know that there has been opposition to the holiday home scheme. The local environmental pressure groups have been against it, of course, but the strangest scene was created by some local hippy who lives in the forest. Known to some people as 'the wolf', he stormed into the developers' offices in town and 'blew his top' saying that we were destroying his 'home'. It was quite funny.

## Property Owner

You are someone who believes in doing things properly. This is how you got to be a person of some wealth and influence. One needs only to look at your home or your car to see that you do not go in for half-measures. A new development opportunity caught your eye some time ago, a chance to build in the forest. It should be an excellent investment, or possibly a retirement home, but can be used for holidays in the meantime. You buy a good plot of land and build a high quality, architect-designed summer residence. You are horrified to discover that some of your new neighbours are putting up flimsy wooden summer houses on their plots of land. One of them is even using it as a camping site!

You are also conscious of security. You have heard that there are some rough types around, living in the forest. One can always expect some vandalism with such people who do not respect the law. One of them, known locally as 'the wolf', made a spectacle of himself in the developers' offices and was thrown out while cursing and threatening. You are not going to take any chances: a strongly fenced garden, electronic burglar alarms and perhaps a couple of Rottweiler dogs should see off any such scum. After all, you worked for every penny you earned and will not have your right to a good life disturbed by those who have probably never done an honest day's work in their lives.

# Cindy and the Ball

In the story, Cinderella went to the ball with the aid of a magic wand which equipped her with a lovely ball-gown and glass slippers and turned the mice and pumpkin into coach and horses. There the prince fell in love with her and all was well after some minor complications. Here we concentrate on the problem prior to the ball. The essence of the conflict is that there is not enough of something (here, tickets to the ball) for all members of the family. Such problems often bring out deeper tensions within the family.

## Wife

You were widowed suddenly, with two daughters studying at college (one of whom is now a postgraduate student) and found that your husband left debts you knew nothing about. The three of you faced acute hardship until you remarried, to a local restaurant owner. He is a kind man, a respected local councillor, even though he is not a highly educated or cultured person. His wife had died some time ago and he was left with his daughter, who is younger than your two and is a very pretty, slightly spoilt and naive girl. You hope to make a more cultured and more industrious young woman of her, but she is not taking kindly to advice and the relationship is far from easy at present.

Now there is all this fuss about the Ball at the University, which will be attended by a member of the Royal Family who was there as an undergraduate. The family was allocated four tickets. It should be obvious that the youngest should stay at home, especially as she would be right out of her depth in such company, but Cindy has to disagree, of course.

## Eldest daughter

You are the elder of two sisters, whose father died suddenly while you were at university. Your mother has remarried and you now also have a seventeen year old step-sister; a pretty, but not very intelligent, dreamy and naive girl whose father absolutely dotes on her. He also helped you to continue your studies for your Ph.D., but has indicated that you are on your own after that. He hardly values learning anyway, since he became a well-to-do restaurant owner and respected local citizen, without much education.

Now there is this ridiculous family row about the forthcoming Ball at the University, which will be attended by a member of the Royal Family, who was an undergraduate there some time ago. The family has four tickets. It's quite clear that the youngest should stay at home; she would be right out of place anyway. She has to disagree, of course, spoilt child that she is.

## Cindy

You are seventeen years old. Your mother died years ago and you have lived with your father till he remarried last year. You don't get on too well with your stepmother and her two daughters, who are both older than you. One of them is studying for a degree at college; the other has graduated and is studying for a doctorate. They both look down on you; almost treat you like a servant. Your stepmother seems to find fault with everything you do. You like going for walks, reading magazines by the fire, dancing in clubs – when she lets you. You also like to help in your father's restaurant, which is also a way of getting out of the house. You are very fond of your father.

Now there is this fabulous Ball coming up when a member of the Royal Family will come back to the town where he was a student.

You have read a great deal about him in the magazines, you love dancing, you have never had a chance to be in the big hall at the University and you are dying to go. The family only has four tickets. Those two bookworms who go to the university each day want to be there, of course, even though they would probably just stand there and gape. Your father is a local councillor, so he probably needs to be there. You know he hates rows, but why should you always be the one who gives in?

## Father

Your first wife died years ago and you brought up your daughter, who is now seventeen. She is a lovely girl, who reminds you of your wife when you first met her. She hasn't done brilliantly at school, but that was not your strength either. It did not stop you from doing well in catering and as a restaurant owner and local councillor; you are a well respected citizen.

Last year you remarried, you did not wish to remain alone when your daughter leaves home. Your second wife is a kind and very intelligent woman. You have learnt a lot from her, but you are beginning to find the intellectual chatter between her and her two daughters rather wearing. They are also very snobbish and seem to live in a different world. What bothers you most is that they look down on your daughter Cindy and expect her to do things for them as if she was a servant. It's hardly surprising that she prefers to help in the restaurant to helping at home. The two older girls are at the university and they are costing you a great deal of money. Nor do they seem particularly grateful, even though the elder certainly could not have gone on to study for a doctorate without your help. All they had was debts when you married their mother.

Now there is this row at home.

Stupid business. There will be a Ball at the university, attended by a member of the Royal Family who had been an undergraduate there. The family has been allocated four tickets. You would gladly stay at home, but, as a councillor, you are expected to go. You know that your daughter loves dancing and is aching to go, but she is the youngest and the other two insist that they certainly want to be there. You can see that this is logical and you hate rows, but you are very upset that your daughter is the one to miss out again.

# The Ugly Duckling

The 'ugly duckling' emerged from a swan's egg amongst ducks. His adopted family took him in, but the bigger world dealt very unkindly with him and he had no safe place until he found his own kind. Separating people to be with 'their kind' is neither feasible nor morally justifiable today. Yet strangers are often perceived as a threat and treated as scapegoats by people who themselves feel insecure.

## Mother

Three of your children have left school, in fact the oldest is married and you will soon be a grandmother. As they grew up and you saw the prospect of the house emptying, you and your husband adopted a Somali orphan. He is a lovely, bright lad, loved by all your village neighbours. In spite of his slight stammer, he got on well in the village school, especially in mathematics. This year he started at the secondary school in town, where he goes by bus with other village children.

Lately, you have become very worried. Your cheerful lad has become withdrawn and gets very touchy about any questions relating to school. He has also lost some books and pens, though he used to be very careful with possessions. His stammer has become worse as well. Last week some money disappeared from the kitchen, which he afterwards said he needed for a book, but he never showed you the book. You were beginning to feel certain that something was wrong. Today he said he had a stomach ache. You rang the school to tell them he was not going, only to find out that he had not been the previous two days either, even though he left on the bus.

You are going in to see the form teacher.

# Boy

You are an adopted twelve year old boy of Somali origin. Your mother told you that your real parents were refugees who died. You have grown up in a village where everyone was kind to you, your parents, much older brother and sisters and the village children who went to school with you. When your stammer slowed your speech down, they were patient and did not laugh. You always did well at school, especially in maths, which you loved.

This year you started at the secondary school in town where you go by bus each day. For a while all went well, but the past few weeks have been hell. First some of them started to mimic your stammer. You tried to laugh it off, but they did not stop and you found your stammer getting worse. Then they started to make monkey noises. Next some of them pinched your books to copy the homework. One of these never returned, but you did not dare tell the teacher as you feared it would only make matters worse. You said you lost it. At first some of your former friends from the village stood up for you, but now they seem afraid to be unpopular. One or two even join in. Last week this boy from the town demanded money from you. You refused, but he and two of his friends waited for you after school, punched and kicked you and threatened you with worse if the money did not come. Next day you took mother's money from the kitchen and then lied, saying you needed to buy a book. It made you feel awful. Then this Monday he demanded money again. Last two days you never went to school, just wandered around the town. Today you are at home, claiming that you have a stomach ache. You don't want to go near that school again.

# Classmate

You are eleven years old and have lived in social housing in town all your life with your older brother and your mum. You don't see much of her nowadays. She has several part-time cleaning jobs. After school you hang around with your brother's gang. They tolerate you, but often treat you pretty roughly. School is not going well. You especially hate maths. The teacher is always picking on you and telling you off, while that stammering African boy can't do anything wrong as far as she is concerned! You have really begun to hate him ever since you saw him smile when she was telling you off.

Of course, you are not the only one who is calling him names and making monkey noises at him. Anyway, it's only a joke. It was particularly funny when he lied to a teacher about 'losing a book', when everyone knew who took it. Then you and two of your mates gave him a bit of a fright after school and asked him to get some money from home. They are not short of money anyway! It was not too serious; after all, you get worse than that from your brother's friends any day! It won't hurt him to get a bit tougher, spoilt child that he is. Anyway, he brought some money, so you thought you'd try again this week. He hasn't been to school since, even though they saw him on the bus last two days. Strange boy. He is a foreigner after all, doesn't really belong here.

## Form Tutor

You are the form tutor of year seven in a town secondary school which also takes some pupils from surrounding villages. It's not the easiest of forms with a mixture of village children and town kids (mainly from the social housing estates). You have tried to get them to mix by seating village and town children next to each other, but somehow the class hasn't 'gelled'. However, your colleagues all say that the class is quiet and generally well behaved in most lessons and there is the normal noisy rough and tumble in free time.

You noticed that there are occasional sniggers when one lad, an adopted Somali boy from one of the villages speaks in class. He has an unfortunate stammer, but he is an excellent pupil, particularly good at mathematics. You didn't think it was serious, though when you saw one lad squint and make what sounded a bit like monkey noises you told him you'll have 'none of this'.

There seems to be a bit of a crisis out of the blue. The lad was here on Monday, and then he was missing the next two days. The boys from his village said that he had a nasty cold and you had no reason to doubt it. Today is Thursday and his mother rang in to say that he will not be coming to school today because of a stomach ache. That's when it transpired that he left home on the bus the previous two days, but never arrived at school. His mother seems very upset and says the child is afraid of something at school. His classmates say they lied to you in order to protect him. The mother is coming to see you after school.

# Problem solving and Mediation

There is, of course, no formula which leads to easy solutions to conflict situations. In fact, it is almost certain that we are not so much seeking a 'solution' as a way of improving the situation. Most conflicts are far too complicated for solution as a result of a single action. After all, we can neither change society at a stroke nor eliminate human failings. The aim is to seek those small actions which may increase trust, decrease fear and make some level of co-operation possible. Temporary agreements, small compromises, practical steps to improve matters somewhat are of more value than grand schemes which only millionaires or revolutionaries can put into action. Not that we should rule out the possibility of radical change, nor discourage creative thinking which might actually open up a way towards a practical solution.

No single process guarantees results. However, the following describes a simple four-question analysis which has often been used with success.

1.  What is the problem? What has happened?

Often this question is answered by various accusations. This suggests that the problem is such and such a person. The first step is to describe the problem in terms with which everyone can agree. This could be by means of phrases such as 'there is a disagreement about....' or 'we see that X would like to... which conflicts with Y's desire to', etc. We need an objective list of statements about the conflict, so we can attack the problem and not the persons involved.

2.  How do you feel about it?

Here we are looking for honest subjective statements about fears and anger and insecurity as well as any positive feelings. We need to recognise that such feelings form a vital component of the conflict whether they are 'justified' from an outsider's viewpoint or not. However, we need to make sure that they are stated as feelings and not as judgments. For that reason statements such as 's/he is unreliable...' need to be rephrased and expressed as 'I STATEMENTS' such as 'I feel I cannot rely on him/her...' etc,. In other words, we should avoid using labels and value judgments, but should describe the effect of a person's action on us: 'I get angry when I find the bathroom in a mess' rather than 's/he is incredibly untidy'.

### 3. What would you like to happen?

It is surprising how rarely this simple question is asked in conflict situations. People often spend a great deal of time talking about what should have happened and whose fault it is that it didn't. Yet the simple truth is that nothing will change the past! Instead of sticking to our positions, ascribing blame based on what we think should have happened, we should concentrate on what we would like to happen now, what our real interests are in the present situation.

First, it is worthwhile to allow our imagination to picture what we would like to happen if we had a magic wand. Even if it is a totally impractical idea, it might point to the direction from which a solution might come. It is also a way of bringing real interests into the open. In the absence of magic wands, we need to clarify what are our most important, basic needs, what it is we most want to avoid, what is the essence of our interest and what is less important. From such questions we get a picture what is vital to each party in the dispute and what it may be possible to achieve.

### 4. What could actually be done?

Here we are talking about practical steps, acceptable to all sides, which might improve the situation. It is no use looking for a perfect solution. It is much more profitable to list a whole range of possible options before having a critical look at what might actually work. Questions such as 'Is it just?', 'What would it cost?', 'Whom does it help?' and 'Who will pay?' need to be asked at this stage. All change will cost something in time, money, emotional energy. If it is not worth it.... then the present situation might be tolerable.

Of course, the present situation might be tolerable for one side, but not the other. The hope is that at the end of the process enough trust and mutual concern has been built so that no one wants to leave anyone else in an intolerable situation even if the change costs something. If this does not happen, the person for whom the situation is not tolerable might seek ways to escalate the conflict until it becomes in the interest of the other to resolve it. Here we are in the realm of nonviolent direct action to help the weaker party to move away from an unjust (and possibly violent) situation.

If methods of conflict resolution fail, then the result is often violence or legal battles, or both. In the end the cost is invariably greater.

If some agreement is reached, this should not necessarily be regarded as the end of the process. The action agreed upon needs to be evaluated after a time. It may be that the problem has been modified, but we need to go through the four-question cycle to identify new action steps which might improve matters further. The process itself can build trust and understanding.

Conflicts bring out strong feelings which may make it difficult for those involved in the conflict to co-operate with each other in problem solving. They may have come to regard each other as the problem and communication may be difficult without constant interruptions and accusations. It is at these times that a neutral mediator can be helpful to guide those involved through the stages of problem solving, which were described in the previous chapter.

Mediation is a process in which a neutral third party is invited to intervene in a dispute, not to decide on a course of action (that is arbitration), but to guide those involved in the dispute through a sequence of steps towards a solution which is agreed by themselves.

The aims of the mediation process are to help disputants to:

- define the essentials of the problem
- identify and express their feelings and fears
- listen to the feelings and fears of the other person(s)
- visualise the ideal solution from their viewpoint
- express their underlying interests and needs
- generate a variety of options for action
- evaluate the likely effects of such actions
- negotiate and agree on some action
- write and sign an agreement
- agree to meet after a time to evaluate the result
- if necessary, start the process again to find a new course of action.

So mediation is not about deciding who is right or who is wrong, or who should be punished, nor about what should or should not have happened in the past. The process of mediation must start without any preconceived outcome. Its main aim must be simply to find some way of improving the present situation, building trust and possibly bringing about reconciliation between the parties.

The first task of the mediator is to establish a friendly atmosphere, to reduce nervousness or fear, to explain what the process is about and to agree certain 'ground rules', such as 'for us to make progress it is necessary that we...

- listen to each other without interruptions;

- try to describe problems without making accusations
- do not shout or use negative labels
- treat everything that is said as confidential'.

There is a potential problem with complete confidentiality if something emerges which must be notified to competent authorities (e.g. child abuse). The mediator would need to warn the disputants if an aspect of the conflict emerges where s/he feels that the process cannot continue with complete confidentiality.

Once the ground rules have been agreed, the mediator leads disputants through the stages of problem solving (see also the brief 'Mediator' notes in 'Big Grey and Little Red'.

- thanking them for helpful suggestions or for patient listening;
- rephrasing statements as necessary (from statements expressing accusation or blame into statements about feelings, fears, needs and goals)
- asking for extra information if something is not clear;
- helping disputants to express feelings, needs, interests, goals;
- noting down possible options for action (without judgment), possibly adding some suggestions to the list but without giving them extra weight;
- helping to formulate an agreement, commenting if it seems one-sided or difficult to implement (some agreements are not acceptable, such as a husband agreeing to beat his wife only once a week – all violence must be eliminated by any agreement reached, not just reduced);
- agreeing to meet again to review the situation.

CRESST (Conflict Resolution Education) have many helpful hints for young people getting involved with problem solving and mediation. They use the acronym GLIDE to help them remember the steps of mediation: Greeting, Listen, Ideas, Decision, Ending.

The conflict situations constructed on the basis of the fairy tales all have many facets and real-life conflicts are also often complicated. In many cases the two people involved in the mediation process cannot resolve all aspects which contribute to the conflict, even if they come to an agreement. The process then has to be widened to involve more people. For example, it is possible that Big Grey and Little Red come to some agreement which is satisfactory for those two individuals, but does not solve the general conflict between the whole tribe of Greys and the townspeople. In fact, they might even be treated as 'traitors' by their own side for making deals with the 'enemy'. This can happen even if the people involved in the negotiation process are acknowledged leaders or representatives.

**It is worthwhile to practise the mediation process using some simpler scenarios:**

A.  We get no peace or quiet since Bs have moved next door, they play loud music till all hours of the night.

B.  We lead a normal life-style, the As are complaining constantly, it is not our fault that the walls are so thin. We enjoy listening to music.

* * *

A.  We have no idea where she goes; she comes in at all hours and uses this house as if she were a lodger.

B.  My parents cannot accept that I am no longer a small child. They keep asking questions about my friends, they leave me no independence.

* * *

A.  He cannot be relied upon to complete any work on time.

B.  She never gives clear instructions and then always finds fault with my work.

* * *

A.  He has 'borrowed' my watch and seems to have no intention of returning it.

B.  He keeps bragging about his new things and mocks me because I cannot afford to buy things like that.

* * *

A.  She keeps picking on me and gives me poor marks even when I try my hardest.

B.  He never listens in class and tries to make cheeky comments.

* * *

A.    He makes not the slightest attempt to help at home. I slave away all day, make a meal for him and then he wants to have fun!

B.    She has no idea what difficult problems I have at work and how much I need to relax and get my mind off work.

* * *

# Conflict resolution workshops

The exercises suggested in this publication can be used in workshops with adults or with young people. Whoever are the participants, the facilitator's first job is to ensure a friendly and affirming atmosphere, with the minimum of tension. S/he needs to plan a framework for the activities which encourages effective communication and co-operation between the participants. The processes of the workshop itself should carry the message that conflict resolution and mediation rely on skills such as active listening and need an atmosphere of co-operation.

The workshop suggested here would be a condensed introduction to problem-solving and mediation, which would throw up many unanswered questions and leave many loose ends. It would not be sufficiently long for participants to practice the basic skills required (a much longer course is needed for that), but it would give an insight into what is involved in the process. It could whet people's appetite for further training.

## Preparations

The right environment for the workshop is important and the facilitator should ensure participants are given time for breaks and to digest their experiences. It is tempting to try to cover as much as possible, but usually 'less is more' and fewer items enable deeper thought. Flexible seating arrangements are needed, chairs which can be easily moved into small groups and then back to a circle. Tables are a hindrance, except for displays of relevant literature at the sides. It is important that everyone should be able to see everyone else in the plenary sessions. If the number is too large for a single circle, or horseshoe shape seating, then a double circle can be used, but workshops with more than 25–30 participants tend to get unwieldy. It is also important that the small groups should feel self-contained, far enough from each other to avoid being disturbed by discussions in the neighbouring groups.

Problems may arise within a workshop and it is important that they should be tackled in the spirit of the process which methods of conflict resolution and mediation are trying to convey. There should always be an opportunity to opt out of any activity if somebody feels uncomfortable. It is helpful, particularly for larger groups, if there are two facilitators working together. Not only can they get round to more groups and get a better feel of what is happening in the groups, but if an individual's needs threaten to derail the process, those needs can be addressed by one of the facilitators, while the other continues to lead the workshop for the other participants. Above all, workshops should be places where all individuals are affirmed as being of infinite worth and places where participants try to be open to new insights from whatever quarter these may come.

Workshops thrive on variety of content and facilitation styles. The following suggestions are sample activities for facilitators to choose. There are others available from the resources listed in the Bibliography and relevant websites.

## Getting started

The Introduction is important even if everyone knows everyone else. The main aim is that everyone should have a chance to say something right at the start; their presence should be acknowledged and affirmed by the rest. Where people do not know each other and time permits, a variety of introduction exercises can be used. Such as

> **A name game** – participants can be asked to share their name and something about it, such as why they were called it or where it comes from.

> **A quick round** – begun by the facilitator such as 'my favourite dessert is' ... 'if I were a type of weather I'd be....' something I've enjoyed/learnt recently is...'

> **A more active** exercise is 'the sun shines on', where the facilitator stands in the middle of the circle (with all others seated on chairs) and says 'the sun shines on me and anyone who is wearing black shoes/has glasses etc.' – it should be true for them and everyone else who it's true for has to move seats. Someone new is left in the middle and says 'the sun shines on me and anyone else who...'. Participants can be encouraged to move to interests/hobbies or even to the topic of conflict.

The workshop facilitator needs to explain the purpose of the workshop and to suggest a programme. S/he needs to give all the necessary information to enable participants to proceed with each activity, without determining its outcome. The aim of the workshop is always to share experience and to gain new insights by building on that shared experience.

## Activities

**Conflict Brainstorm** (using flip chart paper and a couple of different coloured pens)

The Brainstorm is a quick way of getting a 'snapshot' of what comes to the surface in the minds of participants about the topic on that particular day. These should be single words, phrases, briefly-expressed ideas about 'conflict' in this instance. Anyone can speak, in any order, any number of times. The suggestions are written up on a large sheet of paper visible to all. There should be no comments until there has been plenty of time for contributions. The facilitator can then circle the negative aspects in one colour and the positives in another (there are usually more negative ones and some may be viewed as either). This may lead to discussion and the facilitator may ask about the possible positive qualities of conflict (such as being potentially creative, leading to the birth of new ideas and bringing people together to find new alternative solutions. The facilitator may ask the participants what impact they think feeling negative about conflict may have on the way we respond to conflict situations.

As a way of moving towards thinking differently about conflict, the facilitator may want to share with the group the Chinese word for conflict or crises, which consists of two symbols - one means danger and the other opportunity.

危机

Danger          Opportunity

- To explore conflict further, a metaphor particularly useful for young people is of an escalator. Ask who has been on one? What happens? Why is going up an escalator a bit like being in an argument? S/he explains that you feel like you're being carried along, the argument grows/insults become more personal… but escalators have emergency stops, how can you press stop in an argument? Children often respond to this by suggesting you say sorry, or tell a teacher. Ask for other ideas and responses, such as:

- Count backwards from ten

- Take five deep breaths

- Move away and do something different. You can return to the problem when you've cooled down (you might even find it's gone away!)

- Problem solve and cooperate to find a way forward together

- Bring in a mediator to help

- The facilitator may want to introduce the idea of using nonviolent communication, for example:

    1. Make an **observation** (rather than a judgment)

    2. State the **feeling** that this triggers in you, or guess what the other person is feeling. (It can be useful to think of this as making 'I statements' rather than 'you' statements).

    3. State the **need** that is the cause of that feeling.

    4. Make a concrete **request** for action to meet the need just identified.

- For example:

    1. "I see your dog running around without a lead and barking *(observation)*. I'm scared *(feeling)*. I need to know the children are safe *(need)*. Would you be willing to put a lead on your dog whilst the children are playing outside? *(request)*"

# Listening Activities (using a large copy of the Japanese symbol for listening)

- The facilitator may want to ask the group what they think active listening involves, or do a short active listening activity such as:

- Participants are in pairs. They nominate a 'talker' and a 'listener'. The facilitator shows the listeners a piece of paper, whispers to them or gathers them in a group, to explain that they should not pay attention, look around etc. The 'talker' then speaks for 1 minute about a topic they're passionate about, or something they've done recently. Then the pair swops over. This time the 'listener' is asked to interrupt their partner all the time, offering their own experiences. The third time you say there are no more tricks and you ask the listener to actively listen, being aware of really trying to take in what is being said and be aware of showing this with their body language. The facilitator encourages participants to share how these three experiences felt and emphasises the importance of listening skills in conflict resolution.

- The facilitator may find it useful to share the Japanese symbol for listening with the group, and ask 'how often do you listen like this?'

Ears - to hear

Eyes - to see

Undivided attention - to focus

Mind - to think

Heart - to feel

# Helps and Hindrances

This exercise starts with everyone taking a few moments to recollect a specific conflict situation which they have either been involved in or they observed closely. This could be some simple disagreement at home, at school, at work, in a shop or bus etc... Give participants a couple of minutes to choose an example that they'll be happy to share with a partner. They then share this with one other person, concentrating on:

- what the conflict was about
- how they *felt* about it at the time
- what actions, attitudes, circumstances either helped or hindered a satisfactory solution (or improvement) of the conflict situation.

This is an active listening exercise, each person, giving the other full attention for the roughly five minutes each takes to share the story. After each person has shared their story, they find another pair to join. As a group of four they do not repeat the anecdotes, but try to generalise about what helps and what hinders successful handling of conflicts. One person in each group makes a list of such suggestions. After sufficient time, the facilitator collects all the suggestions from each group (perhaps asking each group to give only a couple of ideas in the first instance, to give each group a chance, but going round again until the list is complete).

## Conflict styles

(Materials: pieces of paper with the following animals written on: bull, turtle, fox, owl and teddy bear)

Arrange the pieces of paper as detailed in the grid below. Then explain that each animal represents a different conflict style. Explain each style. If you have done the previous 'Helps and Hindrances' activity, ask participants to stand on the conflict style that most often represents how they reacted in the conflict. (Otherwise ask them to stand on the one that most often represent how they react when they find themselves in a conflict).

- *Turtle* – turtles seek to avoid conflict, they prefer to ignore it or withdraw from it rather than offer their viewpoint or try to work through it.
- *Bull* – faces conflict head on, forces through their opinion at the expense of others if need be.
- *Owl* – tries to find a mutually agreeable solution, willing to spend as much time as needed working through the conflict, highly values resolving the issue and the relationship.
- *Fox* – seeks compromise, sees resolving conflict as a matter of give and take.
- *Teddy bear* – values the relationship more than resolving the issue, seeks to smooth things over.

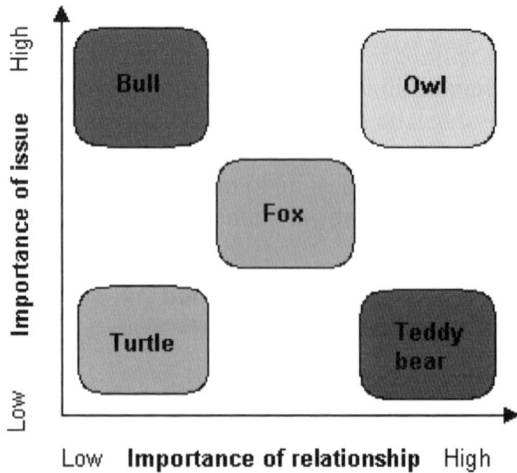

A scatter chart. Vertical axis labelled "Importance of issue" ranging from "Low" to "High". Horizontal axis labelled "Importance of relationship" ranging from "Low" to "High". Boxes positioned: Bull (high issue, low relationship), Owl (high issue, high relationship), Fox (middle), Turtle (low issue, low relationship), Teddy bear (low issue, high relationship).

Low **Importance of relationship** High

Adapted from: http://andrewhong.net/2006/11/26/
conflicts-at-church-choosing-your-conflict-style

Ask the group if they think one style is better than others? Do they need to be able to move between styles depending on the situation? What might be a good style in a situation when people are taking their time to leave a building when the fire-alarm is going off? You might need to raise your voice and be quite forceful – might the bull be a good option? But of course, you wouldn't want to overuse the bull conflict style – it will lead to a lot of people feeling unnecessarily hurt!

What about an issue that's not that important to you, but where the relationship is important. What style might you use? Perhaps the teddy bear conflict style - it can be appropriate to just accommodate the other person, and not damage the relationship over a relatively minor issue. Of course, you wouldn't want to overuse the teddy bear conflict style – it can lead to you giving way on issues that are actually quite important!

Minor conflicts with people we don't really know don't need to become a big issue - such as someone pushing in front of you in a queue. You may not want to create a conflict over this minor issue, it might be better to just ignore it and forget about it, so the turtle style might be appropriate. But of course, you wouldn't want to overuse the turtle conflict style – you may end up being seen as uncooperative!

With high importance issues and where the relationships matter a lot, it'd be best to adopt an owl conflict style. Because you want to preserve the relationship through the conflict, and it's a significant issue, you will be willing to spend the time to get together with the other person, and take however long it takes to get a mutually agreeable solution. But what's the danger of over using this style? It takes a lot of time and emotional energy and other people will not appreciate long discussions about everything!

People often think compromise is the best way forwards – the fox, but what's the danger with always going for compromise? Does it sometimes mean everyone losing out on what they want? Finding win-win situations is the ideal, and this takes a particular mind-set.

## Problem-solving (using photocopies of the fairytales such as 'Hansel', 'The Three Little Pigs', 'Cindy' or the 'Ugly Duckling')

The elements of Problem Solving, which are described in the previous chapter, can be given to participants as a duplicated sheet. It should be stressed that it is one of several approaches and not a rigid formula.

Participants work in groups of three or four, according to the number of characters described. They are each provided with one of the character descriptions from their story and asked to read and absorb it. The group exercise then starts with each person in turn describing the problem (preferably in their own words) from *their* point of view and stating how they feel about it (using first person singular, being 'in role', while not acting out what happened). They are asked to problem-solve together. The facilitator may need to remind the groups that it is helpful to try to discover the 'ideal solutions', the real interests, needs and fears of each participant. They may need to be reminded also that it is not fruitful to dwell on whose fault it was or what should have happened. The aim is to generate a range of ideas about what could be done now.

It may be helpful, at some stage, to call together groups of people in the same role (eg, all the Hansels, all the Old Widows etc.) so that they can compare notes about what has been happening in each group, how it feels, what they think their real interests are and so on. After that, returning to their original groups, they may be able to extend the range of possible solutions, using ideas from other groups. It may be useful to 'de-role' at this stage, suggesting that the group as a whole discusses the problem and also evaluates what has been happening, what they have learnt, what were the difficulties.

# Plenary discussion

This can be used to draw out the key elements of conflict resolution: Co-operation, Communication and Affirmation (skills hopefully practiced during the activity). The discussion can also be related to diagrammatic representations of conflict such as the *Iceberg Principle*. This is a tool which helps us look at conflict in the form of an iceberg – where behavior is above the water, and the attitudes and context lay deep underneath.

**Conflict Iceberg**

Issues
Personalities
Emotions
Interests, needs and desires
Self-perceptions and self-esteem
Hidden expectations
Unresolved issue from the past

Awareness of the interconnection

Describe a conflict, e.g. Michael is 14, he enters his Maths lesson late. The teacher makes a comment about the disruption. Michael explodes. He says he won't bother attend at all and leaves, slamming the door behind him.

Why might they have reacted like this? Might the student's behavior be a result of something other than the teacher's comment? What may have happened to Michael that morning, or the night before? Encourage the group to think of possibilities. Michael also might have 'exploded' because this is the only way he knows how to deal with conflict.

Being aware of the 'invisible' aspects of a conflict will help us better understand why the conflicting parties are behaving as they do, allowing us to find alternative ways to find a resolution. Can the group relate to this tool?

## The mediation process (Materials: 'Big Grey and Little Red' or 'Goldie and the Browns', some of the simpler scenarios given on pages 11 and 15).

- Participants should work in groups of three, using the examples suggested in the previous chapter. Members should ideally try three exercises, so that each person has the chance to be the mediator.

  1. Two of these mediations can draw from the simple scenarios on pages 36 and 37.

  2. The third could use a more complex problem (eg, 'Big Grey and Little Red' or 'Goldie and the Browns') – the other stories can also be used for mediation exercises by selecting aspects of the problem, or by following through a series of mediations, but more time would be required).

## Sharing experience of mediation exercise

- It is not the aim of the plenary discussions to focus on the 'best solution'. This will, in any case, depend on the different interpretation of individual characters and the circumstances described. It may be helpful to look at the range of solutions which have been suggested, but the main aim is to look at the process and to focus on the problems encountered and how they might be overcome. It may be helpful to ask participants not only *what* happened (as they will want to discuss this), but also ask them how they *feel* about what happened/the roles they played etc.

# Workshop Evaluation

The evaluation is important, both for the facilitator and the participants. It can be done individually on a piece of paper (what was useful/enjoyable, what didn't work so well for you/, what would you like to learn more about etc.). We can ask for reactions to each activity (such as a 'spectrum line' reaction: those who found it useful move towards the right, those who did not towards the left), or the evaluation itself can be done in small groups (share something that you will take away from today/what did you enjoy/ find challenging). This can also be followed by a whole group ending, such as standing in a large circle and sharing one word which expresses feelings about the day. Or you could finish with an affirmation exercise, such as:

Affirmation web: (you need a ball of wool) – ask participants if people generally tend to give more 'put downs' or 'pick ups'? Do we find it embarrassing to compliment others? Do we need to practice this skill? How about starting right now? Stand in a circle, say something positive to another member of group (it could be about their qualities, appearance, or in relation to something that's happened during the day) and throw a ball of wool to them, create a web of affirmation.

# Bibliography

*Everyone can win – How to resolve conflict, Second Edition,* by Helena Cornelius, Shoshana Faire and Estella Cornelius. Sydney: Simon & Schuster, 2006.

*Getting to yes: Negotiating agreement without giving in* by Roger Fisher and William Ury. London: Hutchinson, 2003.

*Playing with Fire, Second Edition, Training for Those Working with Young People in Conflict* by Fiona Macbeth. London: Jessica Kingsley Publishers, 2011. More resources are available.

'An Introduction to Peer Mediation – A Young Person's Guide'. This and other resources for conflict work with young people, are available from Leap Confronting Conflict: www.leapconfrontingconflict.org.uk/publications-resources).

*Working with Conflict: Skills and Strategies for Action,* by Simon Fisher Dekha Ibrahim Abdi, Jawed Ludin, Richard Smith, Steve Williams and Sue Williams. London: Zed Books Ltd, 2000.

*The Peace Kit – Everyday peacemaking for Young People,* Second Edition, by John Lampen. London: Quaker Books, 2005.

'Youth Refusing Violence' – a resource available from St Ethelburga's Centre for Reconciliation and Peace. Designed to help youth workers/faith groups/peer leaders design a workshop/series of workshops for young people, exploring themes of, faith and conflict and alternatives to violence: *www.stethelburgas.org.*

*Nonviolent Communication: a Language of Life,* Second Edition, by Marshall Rosenberg. Puddle Dancer Press, 2003.

For more resources, also see:

Quakers in Britain: www.quaker.org.uk/education

Amnesty International – for a range of educational materials on Human Rights Education: www.amnesty.org.uk/

Bridge Builders – training and coaching for church leaders in handling conflict, tension and disagreement in the church: www.bbministries.org.uk

Conflict and Change, Newham: www.conflictandchange.co.uk

CRESST, Conflict Resolution and Peer Mediation organisation in Sheffield: www.cresst.org.uk

Pax Christi: www.paxchristi.org.uk/peace_ed1.php .

Peace education network: www.peace-education.org.uk

Peace One Day: www.peaceoneday.org/resources

Peace Pledge Union www.ppu.org.uk

Peer mediation network: www.peermediationnetwork.org.uk

St Ethelburgas's Centre for Reconciliation and Peace: www.stethelburgas.org

Turning the Tide – for exercises/activities on non-violence: www.turning-the-tide.org

UN Global Learning and Teaching Project http://cyberschoolbus.un.org/ Peace Education Unit: tolerance and respect for dignity and identity http:// www.un.org/cyberschoolbus/peace/frame3_2.htm

UNICEF (resources on children and armed conflict): www.unicef.org.au/ childsoldier.aspx and 'Peaceful Communities for All', an early childhood unit: http://teachunicef.org/explore/topic/peace-education

West Midlands Quaker Peace Education Project (Peace Makers): www.peacemakers.org.uk

Produced by Quaker Peace & Social Witness, 2014.